the little book of
RELAXATION

lucy lane

summersdale

THE LITTLE BOOK OF RELAXATION

Copyright © Summersdale Publishers Ltd, 2015

With research by Katherine Bassford

Summersdale Publishers Ltd
46 West Street
Chichester
West Sussex
PO19 1RP
UK

www.summersdale.com

Printed and bound in the Czech Republic

ISBN: 978-1-84953-787-2

Substantial discounts on bulk quantities of Summersdale books are available to corporations, professional associations and other organisations. For details contact Nicky Douglas by telephone: +44 (0) 1243 756902, fax: +44 (0) 1243 786300 or email: nicky@summersdale.com.

INTRODUCTION

Today's world is more hectic than ever before. Sometimes it seems as if computers, phones and other devices are demanding our attention round the clock, and the needs of our colleagues, friends and family members can feel so all-embracing that relaxation is but a distant dream. However, don't be downhearted: this handy little book is packed with inspiring quotations and simple tips to help you reconnect with your true self and find healing and restoring moments of relaxation throughout the day.

START THE DAY FROM A PLACE OF PEACE

Instead of jumping out of bed and into the shower and the rest of your hectic day, choose to begin each new day by sitting still for five minutes and connecting with your inner sense of calm and balance. Focus on your breath and allow peace to cascade down your spine and flow through your body. As you do so, say these words quietly to yourself: 'I am at peace.'

Each one has to find
his peace from within.
And peace to be real
must be unaffected by
outside circumstances.

Mahatma Gandhi

Nothing can bring you
peace but yourself.

Ralph Waldo Emerson

YOU DON'T NEED TO HURRY

Choose to make today a 'no rush' day. Handle each of your activities with the care and attention it deserves. You'll be surprised at just how much you get done, and at the end of the day you'll feel much fresher and calmer than if you had approached your daily tasks with stress and tension.

Never be in a **hurry**;
do everything quietly
and in a **calm** spirit.

Francis de Sales

There is time for
everything.

Thomas Edison

THINK POSITIVE

Write a list of all the positive things in your life and put it on the fridge or another place where you'll see it every day. The things could be as simple as a birthday greeting from a friend, or as significant as a wedding day or other big event. Whenever you're feeling down, take time to read, enjoy and draw strength from the positive things on the list. Add to it whenever you can!

I have found that
if you love life,
life will love you back.

Arthur Rubinstein

There is no greatness
where there is
not simplicity.

Leo Tolstoy

LET YOUR FACE RELAX

We hold a lot of emotion in the muscles of our faces. Take a moment during the day to become aware of your expression, and notice if you have a frowning brow, a tense jaw or a grimacing mouth. Hold your warm hands across your face for a few seconds and let the tension subside. Your face will feel freer and your mind will feel calmer and more relaxed.

A FREE MIND IS ONE WHICH IS UNTROUBLED AND UNFETTERED BY ANYTHING.

Meister Eckhart

Accept what is, let go of what was and have faith in what will be.

Sonia Ricotti

LEARN TO UNPLUG

Switch off your TV, computer and mobile phone, and spend time doing whatever it is that relaxes you, whether it's curling up with a good book, doing a puzzle or writing a letter to someone you haven't been in touch with for a long time. Taking a break from staring at a screen is a hugely positive and relaxing step – you'll feel the benefits straight away.

Get out of your head
and get into your heart.
Think less, feel more.

Osho

Wherever you are,
be all there.

Jim Elliot

FEEL THE GROUND BENEATH YOUR FEET

It is very healing to give ourselves real physical contact with the world that supports us, and yet this is something we often only do when we're on holiday at the beach. Open your body to new experiences by taking a morning walk barefoot across the lawn and feeling the dew on the grass beneath your feet. You'll step into the day feeling refreshed and strong!

Walk as if you were
kissing the **earth**
with your feet.

Thích Nhất Hạnh

Set peace of mind as
your highest goal,
and organise your
life around it.

Brian Tracy

LISTEN TO THE RAIN

We tend to complain when it's not sunny and warm outside, but other kinds of weather have much to offer us. When it's pouring with rain, find a quiet spot and sit in your car or next to a window in your home. Listen to the sound of raindrops pattering against the panes of glass and allow the gentle drumming to soothe and relax you.

A cloudy day is no
match for a sunny
disposition.

William Arthur Ward

ENJOY THE ORIGINAL SNAP, CRACKLE AND POP

As the nights draw in, take the opportunity if you can to sit in front of a real fire with the lights off and listen to the crackle of wood burning. Allow your imagination to paint pictures in the movements of the flames, and enjoy the scent of the woodsmoke. If you don't have a fireplace in your home, you can often find a welcoming fire in an old-fashioned pub.

Everything you do can be done better from a place of relaxation.

Stephen C. Paul

The time to be happy
is now. The place to
be happy is here.

Robert G. Ingersoll

EXPLORE THE QUIET TIMES OF THE DAY

Get a new perspective on familiar places by going for a midnight walk or an early morning stroll. At these quiet times, when no one else is around, you will have the chance to notice things you look past every day. You may also see wonders of nature that are normally hidden, such as foxes on their nocturnal rambles or bats swooping above you.

LET YOUR SOUL STAND COOL AND COMPOSED BEFORE A MILLION UNIVERSES.

Walt Whitman

Your mind will answer
most questions if you
learn to relax and
wait for the answer.

William S. Burroughs

ALLOW WARM WATER TO SOOTHE YOU

Even if you don't have a vacation planned, give yourself a little me time with a delicious long soak in the tub. Run a warm, scented bath, put on some gentle classical music in the background, light some aromatherapy candles, pour yourself a glass of wine or freshly squeezed juice, slide into the water and… relax.

Sorrow can be alleviated
by good sleep, a bath
and a glass of wine.

Thomas Aquinas

You must live in the
present, launch yourself
on every wave, find your
eternity in each moment.

Henry David Thoreau

SNUGGLE DOWN IN YOUR BED

Make your bed a place of true restfulness by investing in some soft cotton sheets and pillowcases and changing them regularly. If you're able to dry your bedding outside on a washing line, the wonderful scent of fresh air will add an extra-special touch of comfort. When bedtime comes around, you'll have the pleasure of sinking into a blissful cocoon of restfulness.

No one realises how
beautiful it is to travel
until he comes home
and **rests** his head on
his old, familiar pillow.

Lin Yutang

Take rest; a field
that has rested gives
a bountiful crop.

Ovid

ANSWER THE CALL OF THE SEA

If you live near the coast, make time throughout the year to experience all its changing moods. In summer, enjoy the splashes and laughter of people playing in the water; in the winter, when there are no crowds, simply listen to the sounds and rhythms of the sea and breathe in the salty air.

You can't calm the storm, so stop trying. What you can do is calm yourself. The storm will pass.

Timber Hawkeye

THINK OF ALL THE BEAUTY STILL LEFT AROUND YOU AND BE HAPPY.

Anne Frank

Learn to calm down the
winds of your mind,
and you will enjoy
great inner peace.

Remez Sasson

TAKE A BREAK IN THE PARK

Whether you're rushing to the shops or walking home from school or work, give yourself a little time to appreciate the public open spaces around you. A detour through a green space will recharge your batteries and inspire you with new ideas. If you have time to sit on a bench and watch the world go by for a few minutes, you'll be surprised at just how relaxed you feel afterwards.

Rest is not idleness,
and to lie sometimes on
the grass on a summer
day listening to the
murmur of water, or
watching the clouds
float across the sky, is
hardly a waste of time.

John Lubbock

Nature teaches us **simplicity** and contentment, because in its presence we realise we need very little to be **happy**.

Mark Coleman

We must not allow the clock and the calendar to blind us to the fact that each moment of life is a miracle and mystery.

H. G. Wells

RELISH THE SOUND OF SILENCE

Steal a moment of silence in your day. Go somewhere you can be alone and block out background noise with earplugs. Listen to your heart beating, the sound of your own breathing, and focus on just existing. Even if you don't have any earplugs to hand, you can enjoy moments of silence as they arise, such as while you're driving, taking a bathroom break or travelling in a lift. When you free yourself from the need to fill every moment of your day with music or speech, you'll achieve greater relaxation and connection with the world around you.

There are places and
moments in which one is
so completely alone that
one sees the world entire.

Jules Renard

Quiet your mind.
Breathe and let go of
words, worry and plans.

Doreen Virtue

INTRODUCE AROMATHERAPY INTO YOUR LIFE

Fill your room with the subtle scent of herbs and spices to soothe your senses. If you don't have an oil burner, fill a small bowl with hot water and some fresh herbs and place it on top of your radiator. For relaxation, try rose, geranium, lavender or sandalwood: experiment until you find the scent that works best for you.

TENSION IS WHO YOU THINK YOU SHOULD BE. RELAXATION IS WHO YOU ARE.

Chinese proverb

The key to everything
is patience. You get the
chicken by hatching the
egg, not by smashing it.

Arnold H. Glasow

BAKE YOURSELF HAPPY

Spend some quality time in the kitchen by donning an apron and baking some bread. Channel any tension into kneading and pummelling the dough, then sit back and inhale as the wonderful aroma of freshly baked bread fills the room. If you can invite friends round to share the results of your labours, so much the better!

Whoever is happy
will make others
happy too.

Anne Frank

Think in the morning.
Act in the noon.
Eat in the evening.
Sleep in the night.

William Blake

MOVE SMOOTHLY THROUGH THE WATER

Go for a swim, whether in a local swimming pool or at the beach, and enjoy the sensation of water against your skin. Start by feeling the gentle support of the water as you lie on your back, floating weightlessly in its embrace, and afterwards swim with your favourite stroke until your body feels fully exercised. Swimming exercises your whole body, and leaves your muscles feeling relaxed and your mind tranquil.

Remain calm, **serene**, always in command of yourself. You will then find out how **easy** it is to get along.

Paramahansa Yogananda

He who lives in
harmony with himself
lives in harmony with
the world.

Marcus Aurelius

LET YOUR WORRIES FLOAT AWAY LIKE CLOUDS

On a fine day, take yourself to a park or a hilltop, or any open space, lie back and watch the clouds. Your mind will start to make its own sense of the shapes that form and separate above you. You can allow your stresses and worries to float past just like the clouds.

Be happy. It's one
way of being wise.

Colette

EAT WELL, DRINK IN MODERATION AND SLEEP SOUND. IN THESE THREE GOOD HEALTH ABOUND.

Latin proverb

The highest perfection
of human life consists in
the mind of man being
detached from care.

Thomas Aquinas

BOOK YOURSELF SOME LIBRARY TIME

Spend some time in your local library reading or just flicking through magazines and old books. Tune in to the atmosphere of quiet and listen to the sounds of pages turning and people concentrating around you. If there are children playing as they explore the books, allow yourself to enjoy their enthusiasm rather than seeing it as a disturbance.

If you have a garden
and a library, you have
everything you need.

Cicero

Appreciation is
a wonderful thing.
It makes what is
excellent in others
belong to us as well.

Voltaire

MAKE THE MOST OF YOUR LUNCH BREAK

In the summer, try not to spend your lunch breaks indoors in your workplace. If you take a sandwich or salad to a nearby park, the feeling of the sun on your face and the sounds of birds singing and people having fun together will lift your spirits. You'll return to your desk recharged and refreshed, with a spring in your step.

Happiness arises in a state of **peace**, not of tumult.

Ann Radcliffe

A cat pours his
body on the floor
like water. It is restful
just to see him.

William Lyon Phelps

WATCH YOUR CARES SKIM AWAY

If you live close to a lake or pond, why not try your hand at skimming stones across its smooth surface? A calm sea is also ideal. As you focus your body and mind on the task of flicking the stones out across the water, your everyday niggles and worries will fade into the background. If you like, you can assign a problem to each stone, and wish it farewell with love as it skates away and sinks into the deep.

Go into yourself and
see how deep the
place is from which
your life flows.

Rainer Maria Rilke

Everything passes,
nothing remains.
Understand this,
loosen your grip
and find serenity.

Surya Das

SPEND TIME IN A SACRED SPACE

If you have the opportunity, spend some time sitting in a church or other place of worship. Even if you don't normally attend religious services, the calm and tranquillity of the space will allow you to reflect and gather your thoughts. You may also fall into conversation with a member of the community and learn something about their beliefs. Knowing more about how different people look at life can be a great help in bringing more peace and understanding into our own lives.

CALM CAN SOLVE
ALL ISSUES.

Pope Shenouda III of Alexandria

Compassion, tolerance,
forgiveness and a sense
of self-discipline are
qualities that help us
lead our daily lives
with a calm mind.

Dalai Lama

CATCH A FALLING SNOWFLAKE

Next time it snows, go outside and watch the snowflakes floating softly down from the sky. Experience the special silence that only snow can bring, and enjoy being the first to make footprints on an unblemished blanket of snow. If there's enough of it, why not team up with a friend to make a snowman? Sometimes, allowing our inner child to play is just the kind of relaxing activity we need.

Learn to get in touch
with the silence within
yourself and know
that everything in this
life has a purpose.

Elizabeth Kübler-Ross

Confine yourself
to the present.

Marcus Aurelius

BE A CHILD AGAIN

We don't have to be grown-up and serious all the time, especially when we're not at work. Take a step back in time to your youth and remind yourself of the child you once were by watching one of your favourite childhood movies or going somewhere that brings back happy memories.

Gratitude makes sense of our past, brings peace for today and creates a **vision** for tomorrow.

Melody Beattie

The foolish man seeks
happiness in the
distance; the wise grows
it under his feet.

James Oppenheim

RECONNECT WITH THOSE WHO MATTER TO YOU

It's easy to lose touch with the friends we used to know, but it's always worth the effort of making contact again, and it's easier than ever thanks to Facebook and other social networks. Spending time with old friends, sharing memories and catching up is a wonderful way to relax and let your everyday worries slip away.

You're only here for a short visit. Don't hurry, don't worry. And be sure to smell the flowers along the way.

Walter Hagen

Be happy
for this moment.
This moment is your life.

Omar Khayyám

VISUALISE A RELAXING PLACE

If you find yourself feeling anxious or dwelling on negative thoughts, close your eyes and picture your favourite place. It could be a place from your past, such as your home or a favourite holiday destination, or even a place you've never been to. Allow your mind to be soothed by the image, and return to your daily life refreshed by the short holiday you've just taken in your imagination.

CALMNESS OF MIND IS ONE OF THE BEAUTIFUL JEWELS OF WISDOM.

James Allen

Peace is its
own reward.

Mahatma Gandhi

STEP INTO THE SUNSHINE

It's easy to be tempted to stay indoors by television dramas and other forms of entertainment, but if you make an effort to spend time outside every day, you'll soon feel the benefits. Soak up the radiance of the sun and let the natural light from the sky above you brighten your mood and relax away any tension.

The more light you allow within you, the brighter the world you live in will be.

Shakti Gawain

Turn your face to the
sun and the shadows
fall behind you.

Maori proverb

SIMPLICITY HOLDS THE KEY

The acquisition of more and better possessions doesn't necessarily lead to happiness. Instead, take pleasure in the simple things in life: appreciate a child's smile or the laughter of a friend, and connect to the joy that is all around you. Seek to expand your heart, not your belongings, and you will feel much more relaxed.

Wealth consists not in having great possessions, but in having **few** wants.

Epictetus

The poor long for riches
and the rich for heaven,
but the wise long for a
state of tranquillity.

Swāmī Rāma

PICTURE IT

Surround yourself with images that make you feel happy and calm. Postcards on the fridge or a photo on your desk of a blooming flower or a beautiful beach will give you a boost all day. Display your favourite images in places where you'll see them frequently throughout the day.

Look at a tree, a flower,
a plant… Allow nature
to teach you stillness.

Eckhart Tolle

There is a calmness
to a life lived in
gratitude, a quiet joy.

Ralph H. Blum

SOMETIMES A HUG IS ALL YOU NEED

Body contact releases oxytocin, which can reduce stress hormones and help to elevate your mood. Share a warm hug with your loved ones or a family pet for instant stress relief. Take the opportunity to express your love to those who are closest to you through touch whenever you can, and feel your tension melt away.

THE IDEAL OF CALM EXISTS IN A SITTING CAT.

Jules Renard

Let peace be your
middle name.

Ntathu Allen

I LIKE TO MOVE IT, MOVE IT

Exercise not only makes you strong and healthy, it can also relieve tension in the body and boost your mood for hours afterwards. Go for an invigorating run, swim or bike ride to release any built-up stress. If you don't have a lot of time for exercise, even a ten-minute walk will help you to relax and release any tension.

A well-spent day
brings happy sleep.

Leonardo da Vinci

Try to be like the turtle –
at ease in your own shell.

Bill Copeland

TIDY UP AND WIND DOWN

You can escape the stress caused by mess by cleaning and organising the spaces around you. As well as throwing out unwanted rubbish, you can also help people in need by donating your unwanted things to charity. Your new, bright and airy surroundings will help you approach each day with a relaxed frame of mind.

Radiate peace. Who knows? The **peace** you spread may create the only **restful** place in your environment.

Stella Payton

Be the calm centre in
the raging flow of life.

Leo Babauta

SAY 'YES' TO YOGA

The ancient art of yoga has helped people relieve stress for centuries. Not only is it a gentle form of exercise, which will help you feel calmer, but it can also be very beneficial in releasing tension from the body. Yoga combines movements with breathing, so that the mind is focused on what the body is doing. This physical focus helps the mind to relax and stop thinking about the worries of the day. Why not try a class local to you, or look for tutorials online?

Every breath we take,
every step we make,
can be filled with peace,
joy and serenity.

Thích Nhất Hạnh

The pursuit, even of the
best things, ought to
be calm and tranquil.

Cicero

ALLOW YOURSELF TO SAY 'NO'

Many of us feel under pressure to say 'yes' whenever we're asked to do something, and sometimes this can make us feel detached from our own needs and desires. Remember: it is OK to say 'no'. Refraining from overcommitting ourselves allows us to be free of a lot of unnecessary stress and guilt, and allows us to lead a more relaxed way of life.

THE TIME TO RELAX IS WHEN YOU DON'T HAVE TIME FOR IT.

Sydney J. Harris

Without accepting the fact that everything changes, we cannot find perfect composure.

Shinichi Suzuki

Don't take tomorrow
to bed with you.

Norman Vincent Peale

PUT IT IN A LIST

Instead of chewing over your worries all evening, make a list of your tasks for tomorrow at the end of your working day, putting the top priorities first. Doing this will enable you to turn off your 'work mind' and allow yourself to relax for the evening.

Stop a **moment**,
cease your work,
look around you.

Leo Tolstoy

When we are unable to
find tranquillity within
ourselves, it is useless
to seek it elsewhere.

François de La Rochefoucauld

SCHEDULE IN SOME FUN!

Life is not all about work, work, work. Plan some fun into your schedule, and keep your appointments with yourself! Making time to do the things we enjoy, such as painting, reading, walking or catching up with friends, is key to leading a balanced and relaxed life.

The greatest healing
therapy is friendship
and love.

Hubert Humphrey

Never hurry and
never worry!

E. B. White

MASSAGE THE STRESS AWAY

Tension sneaks up on us, gradually and almost imperceptibly tightening our muscles, until our bodies are tied up in knots. During the day, use your fingertips to massage your scalp and the back of your neck with circular movements to ease the build-up of tension. And every now and then, treat yourself to a professional massage and allow the stress to melt out of your whole body.

YOU CANNOT PERCEIVE BEAUTY BUT WITH A SERENE MIND.

Henry David Thoreau

The best response to
any difficult situation
is to keep your calm.

Lailah Gifty Akita

BREATHE RELAXATION INTO YOUR DAY

At several moments throughout the day, be still and take some deep breaths, focusing on the movement of your abdomen as it rises and falls. This will slow your heart rate and soothe your mind. Focusing on your breathing allows you to realign yourself into the present moment, before you continue your day's activities feeling more relaxed and balanced.

Meditation is the tongue
of the soul and the
language of our spirit.

Jeremy Taylor

One way to break up
any kind of tension is
good deep breathing.

Byron Nelson

SMILE AND THE WORLD SMILES WITH YOU

Commit to a 'no negativity' day where you look out for both big and small ways to practise gratitude, avoid grumbling and focus on positives with a smile. Acknowledge accomplishments – both yours and others' – and be an inspiration to those around you. Repeat again the next day.

Sometimes your **joy**
is the source of your
smile, but sometimes
your **smile** can be the
source of your joy.

Thich Nhat Hanh

Humour is the great
thing, the saving thing.

Mark Twain

WRITE IT DOWN

Sometimes a busy mind can feel overwhelming, especially at night when you're trying to sleep and thoughts are whirling round your head. Keep a diary to express your thoughts and gratitude, and notice how focusing on the positive eases life's stresses. The routine of writing each night will become a relaxing part of your bedtime rituals, and will allow you to 'close' each day with kindness to yourself and others.

Nothing is a waste
of time if you use the
experience wisely.

Auguste Rodin

One of the secrets of a
long and fruitful life is
to forgive everybody
everything every night
before you go to bed.

Bernard Baruch

BRING THE OUTDOORS INDOORS

Even if we need to spend a lot of time inside to achieve our daily tasks, we can bring a little green magic into our surroundings. By adding potted plants and vases of freshly cut flowers to our rooms, we can create a restful haven in which to work or relax.

FLOWERS ARE RESTFUL TO LOOK AT. THEY HAVE NEITHER EMOTIONS NOR CONFLICTS.

Sigmund Freud

A ruffled mind makes
a restless pillow.

Charlotte Brontë

MAKE A RELAXATION PLAYLIST

Collect together your favourite pieces of relaxing music so that they are accessible when you need some moments of soothing sound. You can carry your chill-out playlist with you on a phone or iPod, so it's ready at a moment's notice when you're on the move.

The body is like a piano, and happiness is like music. It is needful to have the instrument in good order.

Henry Ward Beecher

It's never too late –
never too late to
start over, never too
late to be happy.

Jane Fonda

TRY A CUP OF SOMETHING SOOTHING

With a herbal tea infusion in your mug, your tea break becomes an opportunity to relax and balance your health instead of a race for the next all-too-brief caffeine boost. Try a mixture of camomile, fennel and mallow for a relaxing drink, or aniseed, cardamom and liquorice to cleanse and revive.

A man of **calm** is like a shady tree. People who need **shelter** come to it.

Toba Beta

He who would be serene
and pure needs but one
thing – detachment.

Meister Eckhart

GO WALKING IN THE FOREST

Take a walk in a woodland or other green area and bring all your senses to the process. Be aware of your movements, the continually changing sky overhead, the mud squelching beneath your boots and the myriad smells as they fill your nostrils. Be present with all these sensations and allow the hushed secrecy of the forest to fill you with cool composure.

There is a serene and
settled majesty in
woodland scenery that
enters into the soul, and
delights and elevates
it, and fills it with
noble inclinations.

Washington Irving

Adopt the pace of
nature: her secret
is patience.

Ralph Waldo Emerson

SPEND SOME QUALITY TIME WITH YOURSELF

Step back from the noise and stresses of life and retreat to your own sanctuary of calm, whether it's a cosy nook in your home, a quiet corner of your garden or a favourite spot in the local countryside. Just ten minutes by yourself will allow your thoughts to quieten down and relaxation to enter into your being.

A QUIET MIND
CURETH ALL.

Robert Burton

To sit in the shade on a fine day, and look upon verdure, is the most perfect refreshment.

Jane Austen

IT'S WHAT YOU DO WITH WHAT YOU'VE GOT

Be happy with less – if you are forever searching for the next item of clothing, the next car, the next house then your pursuit and your stress will never end. When you find yourself in the midst of a discussion about the latest must-have item, give yourself permission not to get sucked into the debate until the conversation topic becomes more positive and constructive.

Be content with what
you have; rejoice in
the way things are.
When you realise there
is nothing lacking,
the whole world
belongs to you.

Lao Tzu

Our freedom can
be measured by the
number of things we
can walk away from.

Vernon Howard

GROUND YOURSELF

Stay composed and grounded by bringing your awareness to your feet. Notice your heels, toes and the balls of your feet and feel how the earth supports you. Allow the ground to absorb any unwanted emotions, such as fear or anxiety, and move onwards with a more relaxed mood to your steps.

Peace comes from within. Do not seek it without.

Buddha

LET THE TENSION GO

Worries and stresses make us tense up our neck and shoulder muscles until we suddenly realise we're hunched up and terribly tight. Become aware of your shoulders at moments throughout the day and allow them to relax down, away from your ears. As you do this, you open up the chest area and loosen tension across your whole upper body.

With the **new** day comes new strength and new **thoughts**.

Eleanor Roosevelt

Happiness is a way of travel, not a destination.

Roy M. Goodman

LET A THOUGHT BE JUST A THOUGHT

At each moment of the day, we are buffeted by countless emotions, both positive and negative. Know that you don't always have to pay attention to your thoughts or react to them – sometimes they're simply the chatter in your mind. Freeing yourself from your emotions takes practice but leads, ultimately, to a more relaxed way of being in the world.

The greatest weapon
against stress is our
ability to choose one
thought over another.

William James

If you do what you
love, it is the best
way to relax.

Christian Louboutin

RELAXATION REMINDERS

It's easy to forget even the simplest relaxation techniques in the hurly-burly of daily life, but by dotting reminder notes around your daily environment you can help yourself to remain serene, no matter what life throws at you. Attach a note to the dashboard of your car, on the edge of your computer screen or anywhere else where you'll see it regularly, with a reminder: 'Stay centred', 'Breathe deeply' or 'I am peaceful'.

ALL THE HAPPINESS THERE IS IN THIS WORLD ARISES FROM WISHING OTHERS TO BE HAPPY.

Kelsang Gyatso

With the past, I have
nothing to do; nor with
the future. I live now.

Ralph Waldo Emerson

the little book of
HAPPINESS

lucy lane

THE LITTLE BOOK OF HAPPINESS

Lucy Lane

£5.99

Hardback

ISBN: 978-1-84953-790-2

Sometimes the hurly-burly of life leads our happiness levels to sink a little. But don't worry! This joyful little book is packed with inspiring quotations and simple, easy-to-follow tips that will help you unwind, relax and greet life with a smile.

the little book of
POSITIVITY

lucy lane

THE LITTLE BOOK OF POSITIVITY

Lucy Lane

£5.99
Hardback
ISBN: 978-1-84953-788-9

In a world where we're constantly bombarded by work and worry, we all need a little boost to our happiness levels now and then. This book of inspiring quotations and simple, easy-to-follow tips provides you with practical advice on thinking positively and achieving a more balanced attitude to life.

If you're interested in finding out
more about our books, find us on
Facebook at **Summersdale Publishers**
and follow us on Twitter
at **@Summersdale**.

www.summersdale.com